Totally Creepy Bugs

Peter Rillero, Ph.D.
Illustrator: Rémy Simard

Publications International, Ltd.

Peter Rillero, Ph.D., is an assistant professor of science education at Arizona State University West in Phoenix. He is the author of *Totally Gross Chemistry*, the coauthor of *365 Science Projects and Activities*, and a consulting editor for the journal *Science Activities*. Rillero has taught high school science in New York City and Kenya as well as college science in Costa Rica. As a Fulbright Scholar, he lectured in science education at the University of Akureyri in Iceland.

Computer Illustration: Rémy Simard

Louis Weber, CEO
Publications International, Ltd.
7373 N. Cicero Ave.
Lincolnwood, Illinois 60712

Permission is never granted for commercial purposes.

Manufactured in China.

8 7 6 5 4 3 2 1

ISBN: 0-7853-3862-4

Contents

intro-yuck-tion

Imagine sitting in your kitchen. Out of the corner of your eye, you see a huge cockroach running behind the refrigerator. Your skin starts to tingle; your face turns red. Quite naturally, you feel grossed out—perhaps even angry. You may have an urge to step on the roach, or you may want to run from it. The fact that bugs invade our living space is one reason why many people consider them to be totally creepy. Yet even when people encounter bugs outdoors, in their natural homes, they may still feel creeped out. Perhaps it is because bugs look so different. Maybe it's because it's hard to know if the bugs are dangerous.

Creepy but Cool!

Despite their creepiness, bugs are fascinating. After all, they dominate our planet. They are in our lawns, in the air, and perhaps even in your bed. (Eek!) They live in Florida, New York, Arizona, and northern Canada, and can even be found in the cold continent of Antarctica. While the Earth has six billion people, there are ten thousand *trillion* ants! Bugs come in nearly countless forms and varieties. Some are large, some are small. Some are fast, some are slow. They exist as carnivores, herbivores, omnivores, scavengers, and parasites. So you really can't understand life on Earth without knowing about bugs. Don't be alarmed if you think of them as creepy, especially if this is how you really feel. In fact, this book will even *show* you their creepy side.

But What Is It?

What *is* a bug? Hey, you know one when you see it, right? Bugs are those creepy crawly things. This book uses the common term "bug" to describe any small land animal with a hard external skeleton. In this book you will find activities dealing with insects, spiders, and isopods. All of these organisms are arthropods.

While this book uses the common definition of "bug," entomologists (scientists who study insects) have a more restricted use of the term. They use the word "bug" only to describe insects of the order hemiptera. Thus, for an entomologist, a cicada is a bug, but a fly is not. An aphid is a bug, but an ant is not.

But could you imagine hanging out with your friends and using these terms? As one friend swats away some pesky mosquitoes and says, "Darn these bugs," you'd say, "Well, technically, those are *not* bugs. The term 'bug' is reserved for the order hemiptera." Your speech would probably bug your friends more than the mosquitoes do! This is one reason why this book stays with the common term "bug"—those small creepy crawly things with hard outer skeletons.

How to Use this Kit

The activities in this book are arranged in order from simple to more complex. We suggest that you begin with activities in the early part of the book, then progress to activities in the middle of the book, and finally do activities near the end. Although there is a progression, do not feel that you must engage in *all* the activities in this book. Thumb through the pages and do those that interest you.

Safe Science

All of the activities are presented for you to do with an adult—perhaps a parent, guardian, or teacher. Since some activities can be dangerous, you should *always* work with a trusted adult. There is one additional thing you can do to practice safe science: Use common sense. Be careful when working with breakable things and sharp objects such as scissors. Another reason it is wise to work with an adult is that some materials for these projects will have to be bought. The enclosed kit has a lot of stuff, but some bugs will need to be bought from pet stores or biological supply companies. See the Appendix for places where you can order these bugs.

...and the Real Point Is...

The activities will help you develop observation skills important for doing science and for living life. Observations are the basis of science. Experiments, theories, and laws all depend on accurate observation. Observing is also important to life in general. If you think about it, life would be pretty dull and useless if we couldn't make observations. The activities in this book develop other important skills as well. Some activities will require prediction, experimentation, or critical thinking.

As you work through the activities, you will see bugs in many different ways. You will see that they can be pretty creepy. At times, your skin might crawl. Yet it is fascinating to learn more about bugs. Read the explanations and fun facts in this book. Knowing a little will make you want to know more. Ask questions, read books, watch nature shows, and learn more about biology. Facts are sticky—when you know some facts, others seem to stick right to them. In fact, as you discover more and more about bugs, you just might find that they are not so creepy after all.

Creepy Bloodworms

Grow mealworms, feed them red food, and watch what happens!

What You'll Need

mealworms, red food coloring, small and large bowls, water, measuring cup, wheat bran or other cereal, stirring spoon, cookie sheet, plastic or glass container, apple or potato, safe knife

1. Obtain mealworms from a pet store or from a biological supply company.

2. Make red mealworm chow. In a small bowl, mix red food coloring with a half-cup of water until it is very red. Then pour a half-cup of bran in a big bowl. Stir in the red dye solution and mix until the red color is uniform.

3. Spread the red bran on a cookie sheet to dry. (Keep this sheet indoors so other insects don't invade.) If you live in a very humid area, ask an adult to place it in the oven on the "warm" setting (around 200-250 degrees) for about 20 minutes.

4. Place the dried red bran in a plastic container and add some young mealworms. Every few days cut a thin slice of apple or potato, add a drop of food coloring to each side, and put the slice into the mealworm container.

5. You may also set up a comparison group. Add young mealworms to regular bran. Every few days, cut a thin slice of apple or potato without food coloring and place it in the not-red mealworm container.

6. Compare the mealworms every few days to see if the mealworms that have eaten red food turn red themselves.

Safety

Use the oven only with the assistance of an adult.

What Happened?

The diet of the red mealworms contained red dye. This was absorbed into the body of the mealworms, making *them* red.

Huge Hissing Roaches

The Madagascan hissing cockroach isn't really creepy, but nobody else will know that!

What You'll Need

aquarium or plastic container, peat moss, wood chips, two jar lids, paper towel, dry pet food, Madagascan hissing roaches (from supply company), apple or potato, safe knife

1. Set up the roach habitat. Put a layer of peat moss on the floor of the aquarium. Place wood chips on the moss. Then, place two jar lids in opposite corners of the aquarium. Fold a damp paper towel and place it in one lid. Add a few pieces of dry dog food to the other lid.

2. Purchase Madagascan roaches from a pet store or biological supplier. (They cost between $3–$7 each.)

3. Introduce the roaches to their new home. Place them in the aquarium (inside the container they came in). The roaches will crawl out.

4. To pick up your roaches, grab them just below their heads, in the thorax. At first they will hiss with fright, but they will soon get used to you and stop hissing. If they are holding something, pull them slowly so you do not hurt their legs. Friends and relatives will be amazed and disgusted by your new pet!

5. Once a week, add a slice of potato or apple to the aquarium. The roaches will use this as a source of moisture and food. Remove the slices after a few days.

6. Keep the paper towel in the jar lid moist. Add new pet food as the old food is eaten, but keep it dry. (If you don't, fungus will grow on it.) Every few months, clean the aquarium.

Safety

Have an adult cut the slices of apple or potato.

What Happened?

The Madagascan Hissing Cockroach (order Blattodea, species name *Elliptorhina javanica*) is from Madagascar, an island off the coast of East Africa. It is a great pet, both mellow and easy to care for. Many insects scamper when you put them in your hands, but these guys just hang out. It'll be fun to walk into school with a roach hanging onto your finger! Some students will run in terror, while others will be fascinated.

insects that Suck

Build a feeding station and watch flying insects gather around!

What You'll Need

measuring cup, warm water, honey, bowl, sponge, bucket, binoculars

Make an outdoor warm-weather feeding station for butterflies, wasps, and bees. Brightly colored bowls and sponges may attract more insects.

1. Mix one-half cup of warm water with one-half cup of honey. Pour this into a bowl. Lay the sponge in the bowl. You want the honey-water solution to be just at the top of the sponge to keep it moist. You may have to remove some of the honey-water solution, or you may need to add more.

2. Put the honey-water bowl in a yard or field. You'll want to lift it off the ground a bit. You can turn a bucket upside down and put the bowl on top of the bucket. Leave for one hour and then use binoculars to observe how your visitors drink the honey water. Watch at night for more visitors.

Safety

Pass up this activity if you or anybody near you is allergic to bee or wasp stings. Stay back as the wasps and bees visit your feeding station. They will usually not bother you unless you bother them. Only remove the station when you are sure no wasps or bees are around. Hose everything off outside before you bring anything inside.

What Happened?

Many insects have a great sense of smell. The ones visiting your station may have detected the smell from 50 yards away. Wasps and bees are frequently social insects, which means they live in hives. When one member found the honey water, she told other workers. This is why you might have noticed many wasps or bees at your station.

Butterflies and moths may have also fed at your station. Butterflies are active by day and moths by night. A butterfly drinks using a long, curled proboscis, which resembles a coiled straw. Bees and wasps don't have proboscises; they drink with long tongues.

Fun Fact

Butterflies have taste receptors in their feet! When they land on something that tastes good, their taste receptors stimulate their proboscis to unroll and suck up the sweet-tasting substance.

Hey Creep, That's My Lunch!

Watch ants creep up and steal your picnic!

What You'll Need

paper plates, breadcrumbs, peanut butter, fruit jelly, chair

Have you ever had a picnic lunch invaded by ants? It's not nice. You might have had to throw away food, or maybe you received a painful ant bite. In this activity, you can watch ants without fear.

1. Sit on a chair as you watch the ants and keep your feet off the ground. For lunch, serve peanut butter and jelly sandwiches. On one plate, set out one pile of tiny ant-sized breadcrumbs, one small dab of peanut butter, and one small dab of jelly. Set the three piles slightly apart.

2. Set your chair near the ant colony and place the paper plate down. Observe how long it takes until the first ant finds the food. What happens after the first ant shows up? Observe how many ants eat each type of food. Do they prefer peanut butter, jelly, or bread?

Safety

Set up a chair prior to putting the food down. Sit in the chair with your feet off the ground. Do not do this project if your yard has biting ants or if you are sensitive or allergic to ant bites.

What Happened?

It might have taken a little while for the first ant to find your picnic. But when it did, the other ants in the colony knew soon enough. Quickly, lots of ants came to the plate. Ants like the energy they get from sugary substances, so perhaps your jelly pile had the most ants. The ants carried food back to the colony. This was probably easiest to see when they carried the light-colored breadcrumbs.

Fun Fact

Ants are everywhere. About 9,000 different species of ants have been identified in all parts of the world. There are far more than we usually see. One 2.5-acre plot of grassland in Africa was found to contain 7,000 ant colonies and around 20 million individual ants!

Creepy Changes

Watch bugs change shape and form. What will they be next?

What You'll Need

mealworms, large plastic container, bran meal, ruler, safe knife, potato

1. Purchase mealworms from a pet store or from a biological supply company. Pet stores sell them inexpensively as food for reptiles.

2. In a large plastic container, pour an inch-high quantity of bran meal. With help, cut a one-quarter-inch thick slice of potato and place it into the container.

3. Add mealworms to your container and watch them crawl around. Now, pick up a mealworm. Don't worry—it won't hurt you. How does it react when you pick it up? What does it feel like?

4. Place a mealworm on a plate and blow on the worm. How does it respond? Put a drop of water on the worm. What does it do?

5. Every few days, throw away the old potato and add a new slice.

6. In about one week, the mealworms will seem to have shrunken in size and curled up into waxlike tombs. All the living mealworms will eventually enter this state. In another week, start looking for what emerges out of the waxy tombs. It will be a *good* surprise!

Safety

Have an adult help cut the potato.

What Happened?

Your mealworms eagerly explored their new home when they arrived, but they were a bit skittish. If you blow on a mealworm, it will probably freeze and not move. Mealworms don't appear to like water; when a drop falls on one, it moves away quickly. When you lift a mealworm, it may wiggle a bit, but will soon rest calmly in your hand. It feels a little hard on the outside, due to its exoskeleton, but is actually soft. When it moves, a mealworm may tickle your hand a little bit.

You may notice, when you look at your mealworms, that some are on the potato. The potato adds some nutrition to their diet, but more important, it acts as a source of moisture. When the mealworms enter the "waxlike tomb" state, they have become pupae. As mealworms, they aren't really worms—they are insects in the larva stage. After a while, larva forms pupa. What emerges from the pupa? A black beetle—the adult form of the mealworm! The beetles lay eggs, and the cycle of larva to pupa to adult repeats.

Dark, Creepy Preferences

Are creepy critters scared of the dark?

What You'll Need

sheet of acetate (used for transparencies), ruler, tape, mesh, safe scissors, clear tape, dark paper, insects

1. Roll up the sheet of acetate into a tube about two inches in diameter. Tape it together in the middle to keep it from unrolling.

2. Cut two squares of mesh big enough to close off both ends. Tape mesh to one side and close it off.

3. Put dark paper over half of the tube. Tape it so it surrounds the acetate roll.

4. Put some insects inside. These can be insects you catch or buy, such as crickets, fruit flies, ladybugs, or mealworms. Close the other end of the tube with mesh and tape.

5. Every 15 minutes, count how many are in the dark area and how many are in the light area.

6. After an hour and a half, find the number of insects in both the light and dark areas.

Hey kid! This is OUR 'hood!

Grrr!

Safety

Do *not* investigate insects that bite!

What Happened?

How organisms react to their environments determines their behavior. Many bugs seem to have a preference for either light or dark. Some bugs, such as pill bugs and crickets, prefer dark conditions. Other bugs, such as wasps, are attracted to light.

Fun Fact

Moths are nocturnal, which means they are active at night. Seeing moths by lamps and other lights may make you think they are attracted to the lights, but in reality, they are *confused*. Moths are accustomed to using distant light sources, such as the moon or the sun, to navigate. The artificial light throws moths off; they loop closer and closer to the source until they hit it.

Chirping Down Dark Alleys

Create a Chirp City—a home for crickets—that looks like a giant bug.

What You'll Need

one plastic two-liter bottle, six smaller plastic bottles, safe scissors, ruler, wire mesh, silicon caulk, branches, marker, two pipe cleaners, potting soil, small plastic container lid, tape, crickets, assorted foods, sponge

Your Chirp City will be made out of one two-liter soda bottle and six smaller bottles.

1. Have an adult cut six holes in the side of the main soda bottle. (Cutting holes can be dangerous and should only be done by an adult!) The holes should be just large enough for the necks of the six smaller bottles. In the middle of the big bottle, cut a food hole about two inches by two inches.

2. Have an adult cut air holes in four of the secondary bottles. Cut wire mesh and use the silicon to cover the air holes with the mesh.

3. Place branches in smaller bottles so that the branches stick a few inches out of the bottle. This will give the crickets things to crawl on and allow them to go between the bottles.

4. Put the six small bottles into the holes of the one large bottle. The branches will stick into the larger bottle. Have an adult apply the silicon around the necks of the smaller bottles. Use the silicon to seal the bottles together without leaving large holes. Use the silicon only in well-ventilated areas. Let the silicon dry before moving the bottles.

5. Now make your Chirp City resemble an insect. The smaller bottles are its three pairs of legs. Draw eyes on the round part of the big bottle. The pipe cleaners will be antennae. Make small circles about an inch in diameter at one end of the pipe cleaners. Glue the circle to the "cricket" head so that the straight ends rise from it.

6. Add soil to the big bottle so the soil is just below the entrance of the small bottles.

7. Put the lid to a small plastic container below the food hatch. Put the cricket food in this dish.

8. Remove the bottle cap from the large bottle. Roll up a sponge and place it into the opening of the bottle. When you add crickets to the bottle, keep the sponge moist. The crickets will use this as a source of water. Allow some water from the sponge to go into the soil near the sponge. The crickets you're about to add will lay their eggs in this moist soil.

9. Buy crickets from a pet store. Put them inside Chirp City and watch them grow and reproduce. Keep the sponge moist and give them new food every few days. They will eat almost anything: lettuce, fruit, ground-up dog food, powdered milk, or other foods. Be sure to regularly remove old food so it does not decay. Keep the food hatch closed with tape.

Safety

Cutting holes in the plastic bottles is dangerous. Only very careful adults should cut the holes. An adult should apply the caulk.

What Happened?

Chirp City comes alive as soon as you add the crickets. They will quickly explore different parts of their city. They may have difficulty walking directly on the smooth plastic, which is why the soil and sticks help them move from one chamber to another. You will hear chirping in your city, especially at night. Crickets tend to be nocturnal, which means they are most active in the evenings.

The mature female crickets will lay eggs in the moist soil. These hatch into tiny crickets in a couple of weeks. They resemble the parents, but they are much smaller. They grow in size until their exoskeleton becomes too small. They molt, or shed the exoskeleton, and then grow a new one. If you don't feed your crickets enough food, the adult crickets will eat the eggs before they can hatch. Yuk!

Fun Fact

Crickets rub their front wings together to chirp. One wing is rough, like a file, and the other wing scrapes against it to produce vibrations. The chirping attracts mates. The warmer the temperature, the faster crickets chirp. Scientists have developed an equation to find the temperature from the rate of chirping. Find the number of chirps in 15 seconds, add 39, and you will have the temperature in degrees Fahrenheit!

Lurking Under Stones?

Find, observe, and experiment with pill bugs.

What You'll Need

pill bugs, net, jar, paper plate, magnifying glass (For an optional "pill bug colony," you will need potting soil, a large plastic bowl with lid, push pin, water, stones, and slices of potato.)

1. Turn over a stone and see if pill bugs are underneath. Pill bugs, about the size of a fingernail, like dark, moist places. An oval shell covers them, and they have seven pairs of legs.

2. Scoop up a pill bug with your net or hands and place it in a jar.

3. Watch and experiment with the pill bug. Put it on the paper plate. Examine it with a magnifying glass. Count its legs. Touch it and see what it does.

4. Pill bugs are also called potato bugs, wood lice, and roly-polies. Scientists call them isopods. You can create a home where they can reproduce. To create an "isopod pad," get a large plastic bowl with a lid. Fill it three-quarters of the way with potting soil. Moisten the soil. Using a push pin, add small ventilation holes into the lid. Put stones on top of the soil. Add a slice of potato. Then introduce four or five isopods. If you keep the soil moist and add a slice of potato every week, isopods should thrive in this environment. After a couple of months, you may notice little roly-polies running around.

Safety

Look at the picture of the pill bug before you go searching. Pill bugs are harmless, but other organisms, such as millipedes, can bite. An adult should make holes in the plastic lid. Use a cutting board so you do not damage furniture or counter tops. Slices of potato should be cut only with the assistance of an adult.

What Happened?

Pill bugs have seven pairs of legs and breathe from gills. They have two main responses when they are disturbed: some run, while others curl into a ball. When they curl up, they keep their hard shells on the outside for protection.

Body Parts

How does an ant look compared to a spider?

What You'll Need

ant and spider (or models of ant and spider), magnifying glass, clay, tooth-picks, branches

1. Take a good look at an ant and a spider. The closer you look, the creepier they seem, with appendages and bristles sticking this way and that. In this activity, you will find interesting differences between insects and spiders.

2. Look at their bodies. How many body parts does the ant have? How many body parts does the spider have? How many legs does the ant have? How many legs does the spider have? Which organism has two thin antennae coming from the top of its head?

3. Now use what you know about insects to design your own. Use modeling clay to make an insect with three body parts. Decide how large your insect really is. Use something thin, such as toothpicks, as antennae. Use something wider, such as branch segments, to add six legs.

4. Write out the following information about your insect: What is the name of your creature? Where does it live? What does it eat? How does it protect itself from predators?

Safety

Do not engage in this activity with ants that bite.

What Happened?

There are similarities between insects and spiders. Both have jointed legs and hard external skeletons called exoskeletons. But there are many differences between them. Insects have three body parts (head, thorax, and abdomen) and six legs. All of the legs are attached to the thorax. Insects typically have antennae that help them sense and respond to changes in their environments. Although most ants do not have wings, most insects do. Spiders, however, never have wings.

Spiders have only two body parts, the cephalothorax and abdomen. They have eight legs, four on each side. Another difference is that spiders do not have antennae, but insects do. Compare the two species to see other differences.

Night Flutters

Study the creepy relative of the butterfly—the moth.

What You'll Need

access to outdoor areas with butterflies and moths, net, jar with mesh lid

1. Observe butterflies. They are usually out on warm days, and they like to hang around flowers. What do they do with their wings when they land?

2. Capture a butterfly with your net. Put it in your jar, cap the jar, and place it in a refrigerator for five minutes. Then, carefully observe the antennae and body.

3. Observe moths in the evenings. They like to cluster around lights.

4. What do they do with their wings when they land?

5. Capture a moth with your net. Put it in your jar, cover it with the mesh lid, and place it in a refrigerator for five minutes. Carefully observe its antennae and body.

6. Release the butterfly (and moth) when you are done with them.

Safety

Go outside at night to collect only with adult supervision.

What Happened?

Butterflies and moths belong to the order Lepidoptera. They have many similarities. They both fly, they like sweet nectar, and they go through stages of complete metamorphosis (egg to larva to pupa).

From this activity, you learned some of their differences. Butterflies tend to be more active in the day, and moths tend to be active at night. In most cases, butterflies have more color in their wings than moths. Butterflies close their wings when they land, but moths open theirs. The antennae of butterflies are thin compared to the feathery antennae of moths. Butterflies tend to be much thinner than moths.

Fun Fact

Have you ever seen an inchworm? These green caterpillars creep along by moving their hind ends an inch at a time to their front ends, forming a loop, then push their front ends forward. This is a characteristic of caterpillars of a large family of moths called geometer moths.

16

Revolting Moltings?

See little crickets molt into big crickets!

What You'll Need

large plastic tub with lid, hammer, nail, wood,
sand, paper cups, two plastic bottle caps, cotton wool, water, dry pet food, crickets, cardboard, pins

Insects have exoskeletons (their hard outer coverings). As they grow, they reach a size where the exoskeletons prevent further growth. They need to molt or shed these exoskeletons—a slightly traumatic activity. They slip out of their shells and are left rubbery until new exoskeletons form.

1. Prepare a cricket habitat. Take a plastic tub (such as the kind that contains frozen whipped cream). Put the lid on a piece of wood. With adult help, hammer 12 nail holes into the lid.

2. Put sand in the bottom of the tub. Add small paper cups, lying them on their sides. This gives the crickets room to hide.

3. Obtain two plastic soda bottle caps. Pack one loosely with cotton wool. Add water and put the cap into the tub. This is the cricket's drinking source. Keep it wet. To feed the crickets, add ground-up dry dog or cat food to the other cap.

4. Buy ten young crickets from a pet store. Put them in the tub and place the lid on. Place the tub in a warm place in your home.

5. Observe the crickets as they grow and watch for signs of molting. After they molt, you can keep their already-shed exoskeletons.

6. Create a molting museum by pinning shed exoskeletons on cardboard. Pin them from smallest to largest to show how they develop.

Safety

Use nails and pins only with the assistance of an adult.

What Happened?

Crickets eat, drink, and develop muscle. As they grow, their exoskeletons become too small. It is like a child getting too big for his snowsuit. Eventually crickets shed their exoskeletons, which split in half. The crickets emerge in a rubbery state. With no exoskeleton, they have no protection, making them especially likely to hide. Look carefully for them. Look carefully for the shed exoskeletons as well.

The cricket life cycle is an incomplete metamorphosis. Crickets do not become larvae and pupae; rather, newborn crickets are small forms of the adult. After growing and molting, they become adults.

Waste Management

Watch bugs help with decay!

What You'll Need

pear, safe knife, three jars with lids, nylon screen, rubber band

1. With the help of an adult, cut a pear into three equal pieces.

2. Put each section into a jar.

3. Leave one jar uncovered, put nylon screen over the second jar and attach it with the rubber band, and screw the lid tightly on the third.

4. Put these jars outside in the same place.

5. Observe the jars every day for a couple of weeks. Where do the bugs congregate?

Safety

Have an adult help cut the pear. Do *not* touch, eat, or smell the pears after the experiment begins. At the conclusion of the experiment, put lids on the jars and throw them in the trash!

What Happened?

You probably found that the fruit in the jar with no lid rotted the fastest. Insects, bacteria, and fungus easily enter open jars and cause decay. The fruit in the jar with the lid on it rotted the slowest; the lid blocked decay organisms from coming in. But because the fruit already had *some* organisms on it, the fruit still slowly decayed. The jar with the nylon screen prevented most decay organisms from entering, so the fruit did not decay as quickly as did that in the open jar.

Fun Fact

The adult and larva form of the dung beetle feed on feces. While that seems creepy, it may make *your* life better. As it feeds on dung it breaks it into smaller pieces so that bacteria can break it down quicker. The beetle lays its eggs in the dung and buries it, which keeps flies from laying their eggs. Dung beetles are so useful that Australia imported them to break down the feces from the imported cattle.

Patterns of Death

Take cool and spooky pictures of spiders' webs of death!

What You'll Need

spider webs, misting bottle, camera

1. Find a spider web. Look carefully; they may be hard to see. Sometimes you can see them more easily in the morning because they have dew on them. Use your misting bottle to set a fine water mist on all parts of the web. This will help you see the web better. Notice the pattern of the web. Spider webs may be creepy killing machines, but they are also beautiful works of architecture.

2. Take a photograph of the web. The sun is best for this in the morning and evening. Try to stand so that the sun is behind you, lighting up the web. Don't let your shadow fall on the web.

3. Take photographs of other webs. Compare the different patterns of death. Make a photographic display that shows the different webs. You might also try to use black-and-white film instead of color; black-and-white will give an eerie look to your photographs and help the webs stand out.

4. Now, have some fun and give your photos an offbeat look. Cut out a small picture of a person from a newspaper. Put the cut-out person into the spider web. Because newspaper is thin, the web should hold a small picture. Take a black-and-white photograph of your web as if a person were caught in it!

What Happened?

Spider webs come in a variety of forms. The pattern depends on the species of spider and where the web is being made. Garden spiders make orb webs, usually shaped in circles or ovals, but other types of spiders make webs in all sorts of strange and scary designs. All of them are constructed mostly to help spiders trap insects.

Fun Fact

All webs are made out of silk. It is shot out of the ends of the spider's body as a liquid but hardens when it meets the air. Each fiber is made of two strands of silk.

Spider Stimuli

What will make a spider come out for lunch?

What You'll Need
spider web (with spider), plastic straw, insect catching net

1. How would it feel to be caught in a spider's web? Would the spider know you were there? Take a look at an actively managed spider web and see what insects are caught there.

2. Use a plastic straw to gently touch the web. What types of touches to the web make the spider approach? What touches make it run away?

3. Capture an insect, such as a moth, and throw it into the web. See if the spider eats it instantly or wraps it up to eat later. How does the spider eat its prey? What part of the spider's body produces the silk to wrap its prey?

What Happened?

Some spiders wait in the centers of their webs. Others wait on the sides and stay connected by a single thread. They wait to feel vibrations on their web. Gentle touches that vibrate the web may make the spider approach; these are the same vibrations that insects make when they get caught in the web. If a touch is too hard, it will make the spider think that something big is in the web, and it will hide. If moths are put into the web, spiders will typically bite them and wrap them in silk. If spiders are hungry, they eat their prey right away. They do this by injecting enzymes that dissolve the inside of the insect, which they then suck out of the dissolved body as if it were a thick milkshake. Otherwise, they leave their prey wrapped up for a future meal.

Fun Fact
While many spiders spin webs to catch food, some do not. Spiders such as the tarantula and the wolf spider walk around and capture food.

Fun Fact
Spiders such as the orb web weaver spin two types of silk threads. The first, which is not sticky, creates the basic framework of the web. The next task is to apply the sticky silk, which catches the insects.

The Big Green Glow

How do fireflies (otherwise known as "lightning bugs") glow in the dark? Find out!

What You'll Need

net, bug jar, digital watch, paper, pen, flashlight, aquarium, mesh

1. On summer evenings, you might see fireflies flashing their lights. Catch a firefly with an insect net or with your hands. They tend to fly slowly, so they are not difficult to catch.

2. Place the firefly into your bug jar and observe. Which part of its body produces the light? What color is the light?

3. Use your digital watch to log the time between flashes. Do this for ten minutes. What is the average amount of time between flashes?

4. Now shine a flashlight on your firefly. Log the time between flashes. Figure the average for ten minutes. How does shining the light affect the bug's flashes?

5. Obtain more fireflies and place them in an aquarium covered with mesh. Are there any patterns to their flashing? Don't keep fireflies for more than a day. Be sure to release them where you found them.

What Happened?

The firefly is a beetle that produces light in its abdomen. It produces the glow from a chemical called luciferin. Fireflies regulate the light by controlling how much oxygen reaches the luciferin. Different species use different patterns of light-flashing. The main purpose of the light seems to be to attract mates. If you shine a light on the bug, it will light either less frequently or not at all.

Fun Fact

Larvae of many types of fireflies feed on snails. Ick!

Fun Fact

Bioluminescence is the production of cold light by living organisms. In addition to fireflies, other organisms such as fungi, squid, and even jellyfish can produce their own light!

The Pitfall Trap

Create a trap to catch creepy crawlers.

What You'll Need

trowel, glass jar, grass, Frisbee™ or plate, four stones

Imagine walking through a jungle and all of a sudden falling into a huge pit! You will make a similar pitfall trap for bugs.

1. Dig a hole in the ground the same size as your jar.

2. Put a pillow of grass in the bottom of the jar so the bugs that fall in will not get hurt. Don't add too much grass, or the bugs will use it to climb out of the jar.

3. Bury the jar so its top edge is even with the ground.

4. Mount a Frisbee™ or a plate on four stones so it sits above the jar. Check each day to see what types of organisms are caught. Release the bugs after you study them for one day.

5. Compare different areas to see which areas catch the most insects. For example, you might compare a natural forest area to a lawn.

6. Now invent different types of pitfall traps.

Safety

Work with an adult and work carefully when burying and unburying the glass jar. Do not handle unknown insects.

What Happened?

While walking about, bugs fell into your jar. The slick glass prevented some bugs from being able to walk out. Some insects, such as roaches, can walk up glass walls; if they fell in, they escaped. If you put the pitfall trap in different areas, you can catch different bugs. For example, a forest's bugs might be different than bugs on a lawn. (Although some of the bugs in a forest might be the same as the bugs on a lawn, the forest would have a greater variety.) The great amount of biodiversity in forests is why many people want to protect them.

Fun Fact

You might find some earwigs in your jar. These bugs contain large pinchers in the back of their bodies. Some people used to believe that earwigs use these pinchers to enter the ears of sleeping people and bore into their brains. While this sure is creepy, it is not true.

This Bites!

See which type of mosquito repellant keeps you from ugly bites.

What You'll Need

two types of mosquito repellant, water, soap

Mosquitoes are easy to hate. Just the idea of something sucking your blood is a gross-out! The next time you go outside during skeeter season, try an experiment.

1. Have your parents or guardians supply two types of mosquito repellants.

2. Put one brand on the left side of your body, including your arms and legs. (Keep the repellant away from your eyes, nose, and mouth.) Put the other brand on the right side of your body.

3. Wash your hands well.

4. Engage in your normal outdoor activities.

5. When you enter the house, locate mosquito bites. Count the number of mosquito bites on your left side and the number on your right side. See if one brand was more effective.

Safety
Do NOT engage in this activity if you are allergic to mosquitoes or repellants. Keep mosquito repellant out of your eyes and mouth. Only use repellants approved by parents or guardians. Children should not use adult insect repellants that contain DEET; there are safer repellants formulated especially for kids.

What Happened?
Mosquitos love people—and their blood. Mosquito repellants contain substances that repel or confuse mosquitoes. DEET (N, N-diethyl meta-toluamide) is a common chemical in many repellants; it is effective for adults and lasts a long time. Some repellants contain citronella oil. This oil repels mosquitoes, but it may not last as long or be as effective as products that contain DEET.

Fun Fact
Only female mosquitoes bite. They use the blood to nourish their eggs.

Cold-Blooded

Do bugs like the heat? The cold?

What You'll Need

bug net, tall clear plastic cup, thermometer, mesh, paper, pencil, refrigerator

1. Use your bug net to capture an insect.

2. Place your insect in a tall clear plastic cup. Place a thermometer in the cup and cover the cup with mesh.

3. Record the temperature and observe the activity of the insect.

4. Put the cup into the refrigerator until it is 15°F cooler than the first temperature. Observe the behavior of the bug. Has it changed?

5. Repeat the entire process at a temperature 15° cooler.

6. Put the insect (still in the cup) back into its home environment.

7. Remove the plastic lid. Observe how long it takes for the insect to leave the cup.

What Happened?

Insects do not maintain a constant body temperature, as people and other mammals do. For example, people maintain a 98.6°F temperature. This temperature is fairly constant, even in cold or warm weather. For this reason, we are called warm-blooded, or *endothermic*. The body temperatures of insects, however, are highly influenced by their environments. If the weather is warm, their body temperatures are warm. If it is cold, so are they. When their bodies become cold, they slow down and may even stop. Insects and reptiles are cold-blooded, or *ectothermic*.

Fun Fact

Cold-blooded organisms need less food when it is cold because their activity slows.

Fun Fact

The hawk moth's body temperature is the same as the air when it is at rest. When this huge moth flies, its wings work hard and create a lot of heat. Thus, when it flies, its body temperature is much warmer than the air.

Worm Bowl

Pick a winner in the Worm Bowl!

What You'll Need

partners, mealworms, paper plates, magic markers, poster paper, ruler, small plastic bowl, stopwatch or watch with second hand

1. Do you think a bowl full of wriggling worms turned upside down is gross? In this activity, you will turn the bowl over to see which worm crawls the fastest. Welcome to the Worm Bowl! Get ready to rumble!

2. This activity works best with three or more people. Give five mealworms on paper plates to each person playing.

3. Ask the participants to observe their mealworms and choose one they'd like to enter the race. Using markers, each person places a distinctive mark on the abdomen of his or her mealworm.

4. On a large sheet of poster paper, draw a circle 12 inches in diameter.

5. Place a small plastic bowl in the center of the circle. Put all contestants into the bowl. Then turn the bowl upside down in the center of the circle.

6. Wait 15 seconds and lift up the bowl.

7. See which mealworm takes the shortest time to get to the outer circle. The speediest worm wins the Worm Bowl!

What Happened?

The Worm Bowl requires observation and prediction. The contestants observe their mealworms and try to choose some characteristics that they believe will make them leave the circle the fastest. When they select a mealworm, they are predicting which will go the fastest to the outer part of the circle.

Of course, mealworms are living things. They can be very active one moment and calm the next. It can be very hard to predict the winner, which is what makes the Worm Bowl so exciting!

Fun Fact

Although mealworms are long, all three pairs of legs are located on the thorax, very close to the head.

Preying on Flies

Watch the totally weird-looking praying mantis hunt down and gobble up fruit flies!

What You'll Need

praying mantis egg cases, wingless fruit flies, and fruit fly food (from biological supply company), small aquarium or plastic containers, soil, branch, seeds (optional), small disposable cup, safe scissors, water, nylon screen cover

1. Order praying mantis egg cases, wingless fruit flies, and food from a biological supply company (see appendix for addresses).

2. Place a one-inch layer of soil into the aquarium. Place the branch so the praying mantis can walk and hang from it. On the back strip of the tank, you may want to plant some seeds. When they grow, they will add background to your tank and give your mantis more options for hunting and hiding. Follow the instructions on the seeds for how to plant them and give them enough water and light. (Make sure your plants do not get *too* tall, or they may push the lid off the tank.)

3. Mantises need living food. In this project, they will eat fruit flies. You will need a soft, flexible disposable cup (not a hard, clear plastic one) in which to place the flies. Cut the cup so that it is 1¼ inches tall. Place the cup in one corner of the aquarium. Move the soil away and place the bottom of the cup on the bottom of the tank. Move the soil back so that it surrounds the cup.

4. When the package from the supply company arrives, add one plastic vial of fruit fly food to the plastic cup in the aquarium. Then add one vial of water to the cup.

5. Hang the mantis egg case from the glass in the aquarium or from a branch. Cover the aquarium with a screen. Be sure that it fits tightly, or your mantises will escape!

6. From the plastic container containing the fruit flies, pour eight fruit flies onto the fruit fly food in the plastic cup in the aquarium. The flies will eat (and lay eggs inside) the food. The eggs will hatch into larvae, which will eat the food and then climb the walls of the cup and aquarium to become non-moving pupae. The pupae will turn into adult fruit flies. The fruit flies will be a constant food supply for the mantises. Keep the original plastic container with the fruit flies; you may need to add more flies to the aquarium to ensure enough food.

7. When the mantis' egg case hatches, the baby emerges headfirst. The babies will be soft until they grow exoskeletons. You may get from 50 to 100 hatchlings! If you get this many, move some (after a few days) to other containers. If conditions get too crowded, you will see mantises eat other mantises—a *very* creepy sight.

8. Observe the mantises. Do their bodies differ from those of other insects? Observe their hunting and feeding behaviors. As your mantises grow, catch bigger insects (baby crickets are nice) to feed them.

Safety

Be careful when using scissors.

What Happened?

The praying mantis is a great "sit and wait" hunter. Its triangle-shaped head has big eyes. It can turn its head 180 degrees to keep track of what is going on. It will stay very still, wait for its prey, and attack with lightning speed. With a quick thrust, it uses its front legs to capture and eat its meal. The front legs are similar to arms. If you have a good source of fruit flies, your mantis will grow, and, in about two weeks, it will shed its exoskeleton and grow a new one. This is called *molting*.

Fun Fact

The praying mantis (order Manteodea) gets its name because its front legs have sharp spines used for grasping its meals. The way it holds these legs in a folded position makes it look like it is saying a prayer. Praying mantises are a protected species in many states because they capture and kill harmful insects. Do *not* catch wild mantises.

Fun Fact

Your mantis home is a mini-ecosystem. It contains producers (plant food material for fruit flies), herbivores (fruit flies), and carnivores (praying mantises).

Fun Fact

The praying mantis is so respected that a form of kung fu martial arts was developed to follow the movement and attack style of the mantis.

Goldenrods with Gall

Insect larvae live inside the ball-like growths on goldenrods!

What You'll Need
field with goldenrod plants, safe scissors, tweezers, nylon mesh, rubber bands

Fly and moth larvae frequently infect goldenrod plants, producing large shapes (like balls or ovals) called galls. To visualize this, think of larva entering your arm and swelling it to the size of a football!

1. Go into a goldenrod field and observe these galls. Count how many are on one plant and how many plants are infected.

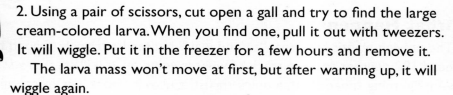

2. Using a pair of scissors, cut open a gall and try to find the large cream-colored larva. When you find one, pull it out with tweezers. It will wiggle. Put it in the freezer for a few hours and remove it. The larva mass won't move at first, but after warming up, it will wiggle again.

3. Put nylon mesh around the gall. For round galls, do this in April or May; for oval galls, do it in August or September. Attach the mesh above and below the gall with rubber bands so that an insect cannot leave the netting after exiting the gall. Check your mesh net every week. What type of insect emerged from the gall?

Safety
Only cut the gall with adult supervision.

What Happened?
You will usually find only one gall on each plant. The number of infected plants varies from place to place. Since females lay about 70 eggs, the number of plants infected can be high. For example, one scientist collected 1,000 plants and found 264 with ball-shaped galls. The type of insect depends on the shape of the gall. Round galls contain fly larvae, while oval galls hold moth larvae. The larvae can withstand freezing because they have glycerol in the blood that acts like antifreeze!

Fun Fact
The goldenrod gall fly (*Eurosta solidaginis*) lives only for about one week after emerging from the gall.

Deadly Doodlebugs

Observe the deadly ant lion larva snare an ant!

What You'll Need

ant lion hole, live ants, tweezers, garden gloves, tea strainer

Ant lions are the larvae of insects called doodlebugs. These larvae create funnel-shaped holes in the ground, which unsuspecting ants fall into.

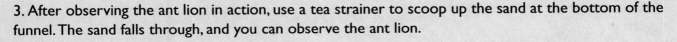

1. The funnel-shaped holes, about two inches in diameter, can be seen around paths, construction sites, and most buildings where the soil is loose.

2. When you find a hole, use tweezers to drop an ant into the pit. If ants are not available, drop a grain of sand into the pit. The ant lion may be fooled into thinking it is an ant.

3. After observing the ant lion in action, use a tea strainer to scoop up the sand at the bottom of the funnel. The sand falls through, and you can observe the ant lion.

4. Release the ant lion and watch it build a pit of death!

Safety

Don't use your hands to pick up ants that can bite! Wear garden gloves when using the strainer.

What Happened?

The ant lion builds its trap in loose soil. Sometimes it will build traps under ledges of buildings to prevent rainwater from entering. The ant lion will often hurl sand at the ant to make it fall into its pit. It then attacks the ant with long, sharp jaws, injecting poison and enzymes. Finally, the ant lion sucks out the inside of the ant.

When you scoop up the ant lion, you will see what makes it such an efficient killer of ants. These ant lions are truly creepy! They have bristles everywhere, and their two huge jagged jaws are able to pierce the ant, inject poison, and suck out the juices.

Fun Fact

Ant lions are larvae of the adult doodlebug. They resemble dragonflies.

Eaten Alive!

Capture aphids and a ladybug. Then watch the bug eat the aphids alive!

What You'll Need

ladybug, aquarium, nylon mesh, aphids, safe pruning knife, cup, water

1. Capture a ladybug and place it into an aquarium and cover with the mesh. Find a plant that has aphids. (Look near the growing tip. This is where aphids tend to congregate.)

2. Cut a long section of a plant stem with aphids at its tip. Place the cut end into a cup of water and put the stem into the aquarium.

3. Watch the ladybug. In time, it will approach and land on the stem. Observe it eating the aphids.

4. Release the ladybug.

Safety
Use caution when cutting the stem.

What Happened?
The aphids are attached near the tip because this new growth is a tender part of the plant. They insert their strawlike proboscises into the stem and suck nutrients from the plant. The ladybug lands on the stem and then travels toward the tip. On its way, it seizes and devours the aphids. Ladybugs are valuable because aphids can damage plants.

Fun Fact
A female ladybug can eat as many as 75 aphids in one day.

Fun Fact
The larvae of ladybugs look like small alligators. Even as larvae, they also feed on aphids.

Appendix

Places to order Bugs and Materials

BioQuip Products
17803 LaSalle Avenue
Gardena, CA 90248-3602
310-324-0620
www.bioquip.com
e-mail: bioquip@aol.com
Source for all equipment

Carolina Biological Supply Company
2700 York Road
Burlington, NC 27215
800-334-5551
www.carosci.com
e-mail: carolina@carolina.com
Source for most bugs and equipment

Grubco
P.O. Box 15001
Hamilton, OH 45015
800-222-3563
www.wherp.com/grubco
e-mail: grubco@herp.com
Source for inexpensive mealworms and crickets

Insect Lore
P.O. Box 1535
Shafter, CA 93263
800-LIVE-BUG
www.insectlore.com
e-mail: insect@lightspeed.net
Source for many bugs and some equipment

Rainbow Mealworms and Crickets
P.O. Box 4907
126 East Spruce Street
Compton, CA 90220
800-777-9676
www.rainbowmealworms.com
e-mail: order@rainbowmealworms.com
Source for inexpensive mealworms, crickets, hissing roaches, and other insects

Ward's Natural Science Establishment
P.O. Box 1712
Rochester, NY 14603
800-962-2660
www.wardsci.com
Source for most bugs and equipment

World Wide Web Sites of Interest

Arthropod Proverbs
gnv.ifas.ufl.edu/~entweb/proverbs.htm

The Bug Club
www.ex.ac.uk/bugclub

Children's Butterfly Site
www.mesc.usgs.gov/butterfly/Butterfly.html

Entomological Society of America
www.entsoc.org

Sonoran Arthropod Studies Institute
www.sasionline.org

Young Entomologists' Society
members.aol.com/YESbugs/bugclub.html

Glossary

For words that "bug" you

Antennae: Long, slender sensory detectors on the heads of insects and crustaceans.

Arthropod: A phylum of organisms that have segmented bodies with exoskeletons with no backbones. Arthropods include insects, crustaceans, and arachnids.

Bioluminescence: The production of a cold light by living organisms (such as the firefly).

Carnivore: An organism that consumes *only* animals or animal materials.

Caterpillar: The larva of a moth or butterfly.

Cephalothorax: The part of spiders and crabs that contains a fused head and thorax.

Complete Metamorphosis: The life cycle of insects in the sequence of egg, larva, pupa, and adult.

Decay: The process where once-living things are broken down into simpler molecules.

Decomposer: An organism assisting the process of decay by feeding on dead organisms or products from dead organisms.

Dominant: A gene is dominant if its trait is expressed when it is paired with a different gene.

Ectothermic: Cold-blooded organisms whose internal body temperatures are influenced by the environment.

Egg: A round or oval object produced by living things that contains the stuff to produce a new life.

Endothermic: Warm-blooded organisms whose bodies control their own temperatures.

Entomologist: A person who studies insects.

Exoskeleton: The hard outer covering of an arthropod, made of chitin.

Gall: An abnormal growth on plants due to the presence of another organism.

Genetics: The study of heredity.

Hatchling: The newborn organism that emerges from an egg.

Herbivore: An organism that consumes only plants or plant materials.

Incomplete Metamorphosis: The life cycle of insects that do not have a larva or a pupa stage. Insects go from egg to nymph to adult.

Insect: A class of arthropod with six legs and three body segments.

Larva: The immature wormlike form of an insect that undergoes complete metamorphosis.

Maggots: The larvae of flies.

Metamorphosis: Dramatic changes in an organism's structures as it goes through its life cycle.

Molting: The process in which arthropods shed their exoskeletons.

Mutant: An organism different than other organisms of a same species due to a change in its DNA.

Mutation: Changes in the DNA of an organism.

Nutrients: Molecules needed for an organism's energy and growth.

Nymph: An immature form of an insect. Nymphs resemble adults but are smaller.

Omnivore: An organism that feeds on both plant and animal materials.

Predator: An organism that catches and consumes another organism.

Prey: The organism that a predator feeds upon.

Proboscis: A tubelike mouthpart adapted for sucking or piercing.

Pupa: A non-feeding, non-mobile form of an insect between the larva and adult stages.

Queen: A developed female in an ant, wasp, or bee colony, often the only individual to lay eggs.

Thorax: The part of an insect where the legs attach. The thorax connects the head to the abdomen.

Wild Type: The non-mutated form of an organism.